START

WITH

VISION

YOU DON'T HAVE TO BE PERFECT TO BE AMAZING

BY
SUSAN SULLIVAN

STUDY GUIDE

Skinny Brown Dog Media
www.SkinnyBrownDogMedia.com

Published by Skinny Brown Dog Media
www.SkinnyBrownDogMedia.com

Developmental Editing and Design: Eric G Reid
www.ericgreid.com

ISBN 978-1-7370393-4-1

Start With Vision: You Don't Have to Be Perfect to Be Amazing
ISBN: 978-1-7370390-2-7 Paperback
ISBN: 978-1-7370393-5-8 Hardback
ISBN: 978-1-7370393-6-5 e Book
ISBN 978-1-7370393-4-1 Study Guide paperback
ISBN: 978-1-7370393-9-6: Facilitatory Guide paperback

Library of Congress Cataloging-in-Publication Data
Library of Congress Cataloging-in-Publication application has been submitted

The Maxwell Leadership Bible: New King James Version is the source file for all Bible quotes, unless otherwise noted.

DEDICATION

The *Start with Vision: You Don't Have to Be Perfect to Be Amazing Study Guide* is dedicated to every person young and old, that has long known that a bigger bolder life was waiting for them and did not know how to achieve it, until now.

I hope and dream that the *Start with Vision Study Guide* will be the first step in you stepping into who you were called to be and understanding what an incredible journey God has for you.

Remember,

You Don't Have to Be Perfect to Be Amazing

Susan Sullivan

CONTENTS

INTRODUCTION

Congratulations on saying YES to you and your dreams! Today is the start of turning your dreams into a reality. The real investment is the time and energy you will put in during these lessons.

Here are a few tips for setting yourself up for success:

- Don't jump ahead in the study guide. Stay with the facilitator. Everything has been designed and planned out very strategically.

- What you get out of each lesson will be directly proportional to what you put in. So try and leave your fears and inhibitions at the door. Be Present. Play Full Out. Keep Your Energy Up. Step Out of Your Comfort Zone.

- There is redundancy built-in for a purpose. You might hear the same questions or be asked to repeat exercises with slight changes. Flow with it. Don't fight it. Take a moment to approach each exercise and question with an open perspective and awareness that something new might be discovered.

- Your vision and the lesson you learn will change not only during the group but after, be open to those changes and embrace the change.

- This is a study guide. You will be asked to study yourself, your beliefs, and your dreams along with the information between the cover.

- Respect the space, Respect each other, Respect yourself and your bounders. Everything shared is to be kept confidential. Together we create a safe space for growth and change.

LESSON ONE
BUILDING A VISION

GOD HAS PLACED WITHIN EACH PERSON A VISION THAT IS DESIGNED TO GIVE PURPOSE AND MEANING TO LIFE.

Acompany's vision is one of the most important foundational pieces of an organization. It gives the company a direction to move towards and a larger purpose for employees to rally behind. Without a clear Vision, the company gets stuck.

You probably already know this if you're a business owner or entrepreneur. You've also most likely invested serious time into outlining a vision for your business and getting everyone excited about it.

But what about a vision for your life? We often don't think about our life's vision the same way we do a company's vision -- but they are the same. Just like a company's vision, establishing a vision for your life gives you a direction to move towards. Your vision helps develop the long- term strategies and goals of creating a life. Your defined vision can provide you with clarity and can help you more easily control your actions and reactions to create your best life.

What is a Vision Statement?

A Vision Statement describes what you desire to achieve in the long run, generally in a time frame of five to ten years, or sometimes even longer. It represents a vision of what your life will look like in the future and sets a defined direction for the planning and execution.

What Are the Benefits of Creating a Vision For Your Life?

- A vision puts substance behind your goals. Setting a goal without clarity of where those goals can lead to frustration and defeat. However, when goals become steppingstones toward the bigger vision, success is certain.

- A vision makes it easier to get through roadblocks. Roadblocks become success blocks when we lack the vision to see past them. Being vision-focused makes the roadblocks simple, short detours.

- A vision sets your expectations. When you know what you want to accomplish in life, you'll know if you're on the right path and when you are closer to meeting your expectations of success.

Your life vision will be uniquely yours -- which means you need to find it for yourself. The good news is that this study guide is filled with detailed steps you can follow to find that vision for your life and, more importantly, achieve that vision.

What Makes a Good Vision Statement?

Good Vision Statements have a few common components:

- It is written in the present, not the future tense. They describe what we will feel, hear, think, say and do as if we had reached our vision now. When we write the Vision Statement in the future tense, we may believe that it is too far from reach or something that will happen sometime in the future. Therefore, we might not connect to a vision in the future tense. However, when we make the Vision Statement in the present tense, it feels like we are living it. It becomes alive. As a result, our subconscious mind conditions itself for believing and achieving it.

- It is summarized with a powerful phrase. That phrase forms the first paragraph of the Vision Statement. The powerful phrase is repeated in whatever communication mediums you have to trigger the memory of the longer statement. This is not to say you cannot have a longer, more explicit, more detailed Vision Statement. However, you should have a short trigger phrase or statement that you can use to summarize the bigger picture of what you're creating. Like a logline does not tell the whole movie, but it does get people into the theater, your summary statement does not detail the entire vision.

- Your Vision Statement should be challenging. A powerful Vision Statement challenges and motivates you for growth and achieving something bigger. A visionary leader dreams of something big enough to challenge themselves and take them out of their comfort zones. When there is no challenge, there is no growth. For example, the statement "I'll live a healthier lifestyle" seems reasonable. However, "I live in optimum health and be in peak mental, physical, and spiritual fitness at all times" is definitely more challenging as it demands becoming the optimum example of well-being possible.

- Your Vision Statement should be relatable. If you cannot relate to the vision, it is like not having vision at all. The words and ideas held in your vision should touch you in one way or another. When you can relate to the vision with every fiber of your being, you become interested in fulfilling the vision.

- Your Vision Statement should also connect to your core values. A vision that has its roots in your core values will keep you on track during turbulent times as long as you stick to your core values.

- Your Vision Statement should evoke emotion. It is obviously and unashamedly passionate. However, it separates the physical aspect of vision in what we see, hear, and do from the soft aspect of vision in what we think and feel. Therefore, not only should it help build a picture, but it should also create a feeling.

If you try and build a Vision Statement without these components, you run the risk of not inspiring and energizing your goals and dreams into reality.

What a Great Vision sounds like.

"Our restaurant is a place where people come to relax, have a good time, and enjoy a great meal. [The short, memorable summary phrase].

From the moment our customers walk in the door, they are greeted by a warm atmosphere, subtle music, and friendly and courteous staff.

We cater to large groups that are out to have fun, as well as romantic dinners for people celebrating a special occasion. The restaurant is packed full of customers, and yet we efficiently avoid long delays while they are being seated and while their food is prepared.

The lighting, table arrangements, atmosphere, and decorations all encourage our customers to relax, let go of their concerns, and open up to new taste sensations. We provide exceptional service all night long.

When they are done, we take care of their check quickly and efficiently. They leave happy, satisfied, but not overly bloated or full. They leave with the desire of just one more bite of our wonderful food."

How clear is that about what we want to achieve as a restaurant? It doesn't make any statements about profits, it assumes they will come if they achieve their vision.

Your Perspective Determines Your Vision

A lot of people don't think it matters how we see ourselves. The truth is, your perspective of who you are and what is possible will determine your vision. If you see yourself as someone who will never go anywhere or achieve anything significant, guess what? Your vision will take you there, or no where. You will be in the same place year after year. How you see yourself or, maybe more importantly, how you see your future self is where your vision will take you.

Where you are today is not where you must stay. What has happened in the past does not have to determine the future. Don't be that person that never dreams and reaches for the stars.

God wants us to see ourselves being our BEST and having the BEST. There is a song with a line that goes something like this… God has not brought me this far to leave me alone… You have not been given a vision without the resources.

You are Resourced.

Start with Vision is based on the belief that you have been created with a purpose and passion, and with all the resources you need already within you to live that vision. Being resourced does not mean you have enough money in the bank or time on your calendar. Being resourced means that you have all the world at your command.

> *and all these blessings shall come upon you and*
> *overtake you if you obey the voice of God.*
> *Deuteronomy 28:1-2*

Leaning into the vision that is planted in your heart is obeying the voice of God. Aside from the talents and skills you are aware of, there is an endless list of blessings (resources) ready to overtake you. So often, we take for granted the gifts we have, the talents that others praise us for, and the knowledge and wisdom we have earned along our journey. Starting now, know that all this and more are the resources you have at your will to achieve your vision.

The Challenges of Having a Vision.

Yes, there will be challenges to having a vision. Wanting more for your life often comes at a cost. As John Maxwell says, "Everything worthwhile is uphill." No one said it was going to be easy. But it's totally worth it. You will have to break old habits and establish new ones. You will have to set new priorities for your time. You will have to leave some friends and maybe even family behind as you venture out into the new vision of your life. And probably the most challenging thing is you will have to accept that not everyone will support you in your quest for a better, bigger life. Telling you it will not be easy is not an excuse to stop but to let you know that every person you admire that is living a big dream has faced the challenges you are about to face. But because they held to their vision, they succeeded, and you will too.

Because they believed in themselves and their vision, they overcame the setback, and you will too. When holding your vision gets hard, just remember God planted that vision in you, and He will see you fulfill that vision and more than you can imagine.

EXERCISES FOR LESSON 1

Exercise 1

Brain Dump: Build an *"I want ... in my lift"* list.

Take a moment and settle in, close your eyes and just breathe for a moment. When you open your eyes, I want you to fill the page with as many "I want …. In my life" statements as you can think of. Don't let money, age, or education limit your thinking. Be Honest. Be Bold. Be Daring with your list.

____

____

____

____

____

Exercise 2

Building a vision.

Let's start to build a vision. Review your list from exercise one and label each I want…in my life statement with a 1, 3, or 5 representing how soon you want to see that statement fulfilled in your life. It is OK if you are unsure about HOW it will happen. Focus instead on the WHEN you would like it to happen.

____

____

____

____

____

Exercise 3

Vision changes with perspective.

Take a moment and write a brief paragraph about how your perspective regarding "vision" has changed because of these first exercises.

____

____

____

____

____

Exercise 4

I am fully resourced.

Close your eyes and just breathe for a moment. When you open your
eyes, I want you to fill the page with as many "I am" positive statements about yourself as you can think of. "I am" affirmations affect
the conscious and the subconscious mind. The words in a positive
self- affirmation like "I am strong", "I am smart", "I am clever", "I am
good with numbers", can help inspire and motivate you to act and
think in a way that will align with your vision.

____

____

____

____

____

Exercise 5

Building your Vision Statement.

Take three items from the list you labeled as one year in the "I Want
... in my life" exercise and three positive statements about yourself
from the "I am" exercise and combine them. An example is "through
my natural curiosity and passion for learning I will complete my
GED." The "I am" statement in this example is, Curiosity and Passion, and the "I want" is my GED.

Try using the format: Through/by/with my ... I will achieve/have/do
...

____

____

____

____

____

Exercise 6

One step in the right direction.

One step in the right direction is how you start a journey of a thousand miles. List one step for each of your Vision Statements you wrote in the "Building your Vision Statement" exercise.

Try using the format: Through/by/with my ... I will achieve/have/do ... with the first step being ...

____

____

____

____

Exercise 7

Knowing that the vision for your life and business you are now starting to build is what you are called to do, and that God wants you to live a passion-filled, big life, how do you feel? What has changed?

Use the space below to record your feelings?

____

____

____

____

____

LESSON TWO
OUTLINING GOALS

GOALS ARE NOT ONLY ABSOLUTELY NECESSARY TO MOTIVATE US. THEY ARE THE FULL OF LIFE AND THE STEPPINGSTONES OF OUR VISION

Goal setting is the first step in moving our vision into action and helps us develop an action plan. Goals are more deliberate than desires and momentary intentions. Therefore, setting goals means committing thought, emotion, and behavior towards attaining the goal. When we write our goals, we will focus on moving towards something and not away from something, and we will build our goals from where we ended in the previous lesson. But first, let's get clear on a few things when it comes to goals.

Why We Need Goals.

You might be thinking, "why do I need goals?" I have a vision. I know what I want my life to look like. I wrote down an action step, and I know the resources I have that will get me to my vision. All that is a good start, but let's just take a moment and look at four reasons you need goals.

- Goals define what we want.

  When we write out our goals, we make a statement of what we want and don't want in our lives and business. Without goals, we take what we get and think that's all there is for us in life.

- Goals help us make a decision.

Decisions are choices based on a set of values. With each choice you face, you are also presented with an opportunity to pursue and manifest your vision. Those choices become decisions that move you closer to your vision or further away from it with a goal. Thus, every decision, from what to eat for breakfast to what career to pursue to how you spend money, is assigned meaning. Goals help us to set decision boundaries to stay in line and move forward. Yes!

Decision making is a huge part of setting and achieving your goals.

- Goals help us be accountable.

Accountability is about measuring your progress. Accountability is not about the task, project, or result. It's about your willingness to accept the role of being responsible for the outcome of your actions. Therefore, it is essential to have an accountability partner when you are moving forward.

- Goals define our success.

Successful people permit themselves to dream as big as they want. So when you create a vision for your life that might seem wildly ambitious, and you take steps every day towards a goal, how do you know if you are successful? Having goals helps us understand that our actions create the results we want, and those results are called success and are measurable.

How to Create S.M.A.R.T. Goals.

In *Start with Vision, You Don't Have to Be Perfect to Be Amazing,* is a very detailed explanation and outline of S.M.A.R.T. goals and give you an example of what a S.M.A.R.T. goal looks like and how to create one. For this lesson, here is just a brief recap. S.M.A.R.T. is an acronym to guide you in setting goals. The letters *S* and *M* generally mean specific and measurable. *A* is for achievable (or attainable). *R* is about making the goal relevant to where you are and where you want to be. And, *T* is time-bound. When you sit down later in this lesson to write out a goal, ask yourself the following S.M.A.R.T. goal questions.

- Is this goal **Specific** – targeted a specific area of improvement?

- Is this goal **Measurable** – quantifiable or at least suggest an indicator of progress?

- Is this goal **Achievable** – is there enough of a challenge to require me to grow and yet be achievable?

- Is this goal **Relevant** – does the goal matter to you, and does it align with other relevant goals?

- Is this goal **Time-bound** – does it specify when the result(s) must be achieved?

Five Things to Stay Focused on Your Vision and Goals.

Do these five things each day to help you stay connected to your Vision and goals, regardless of whether it is a workday, weekend, or traveling on vacation. These daily five can keep you focused and centered on the things you need. They ground and energize you. They help you focus and be creative. Best of all, they are flexible, meaning they all need to be done daily, but they don't need to be done for the same amount of time or intensity.

1. Growing spirituality.

2. Growing your health.

3. Strengthening your relationships.

4. Invest in your career or business.

5. Increase your knowledge.

What Does the Daily Five Look Like in Action?

Growing or strengthening spiritually is about getting into God's word followed by a prayer to prepare to be obedient to His word for the day ahead. Growing health is about what fits and what feels right. Some days, it's time on the treadmill. Other days it's a long walk or going down to the lake dock and stretching as the sun rises. When it comes to being healthy, remember that it is easier to maintain a system than to try and rebuild one. That's why some form of exercise is part of the daily five.

The third area is about strengthening relationships. Ask yourself how I can add value to those closest to me, and then create a list of the other relationships you need to build or invest into. Once you have the people-to-touch list, next, pull out your goals and check in on how you are doing with staying in motion towards them. Next, compare your goals to your calendar and make sure the priority activities for the day and the week ahead support the goals, and what you want to achieve. Number five of the top five is about never "stop learning." You have to plan time for learning in your day. Maybe it is reading a book, being on a webinar, or listening to a podcast. Each day you want to be able to say, "guess what I learned today."

Those are the daily five. Some days, it can take forty-five minutes to an hour. Other days as your schedule allows. There are days you might spend two hours working your way through all five. It's not about the amount of time each day. It's about the consistency and the compound effect over time. Think about what it would look like if you read just ten pages of a book a day. That would be 300 pages a month or roughly 20 books a year. Did you know that most people struggle to read four books a year? Simply reading ten pages a day on a subject would make you 500 times "smarter" than the average person. Now you are starting to see the power of the daily five.

Personal Goals vs. Business Goals.

Let's take a minute and look at the difference between personal and professional goals. Professional goals are related to what you want to accomplish with your education and career. In comparison, personal goals are generally more connected with your health, happiness, relationships, and well-being. Professional goals are essential because, while money doesn't equal happiness, the average person will spend 90,000 hours working over a lifetime. So, you might want to find a way to be fulfilled in your career. Personal goals can sometimes be harder to achieve because the benefits aren't necessarily monetized, so personal goals often take a backseat to goals that have more tangible results. Personal goals are also frequently forgotten - because who's got time for personal goals when you're just trying to survive? But personal goals are just as important as professional goals, sometimes even more so. Personal goals make up three of daily fives because you don't want to climb the corporate ladder only to find yourself miserable, alone, and unfulfilled.

A few last things to remember about goals.

- Focus Your Goals On YOU. This is not about being selfish. This is about self-care. If you are not caring for yourself, you will not be able to care for others. Or, as the saying goals, you can't draw fresh water from a dry well.

- Be clear about which goals are timeline-driven. All goals should have a due date, or they just become daydreams. However, other goals are timeline-driven or have a sequence of what has to occur in a particle order to be achieved. Those goals that are timeline-driven need extra attention on your schedule to be achieved.

- Make sure your goals are indeed yours. When you join an organization or a business, there is always a set of goals and a timetable for achieving those goals that are the recommended path for success. They may be great goals, but they may not be yours. Remember goals need to be relevant to your personal goals and your vision. Not all goals are equal, and not all people follow the same process for achieving a goal on their way to a vision, and that is perfectly OK. Just be you and live into your goals first.

EXERCISES FOR LESSON 2

Exercise 1

What is one reason listed for "why we need goals" that struck you as the most important? Why?

____

____

____

____

Exercise 2

What qualities do you think make a good accountability partner / coach? Who do you know that might help you remain accountable for achieving your goals?

____

____

____

____

Exercise 3

Take the "I want …" statement you wrote in lesson two, exercise six. Then, update them to be S.M.A.R.T. goals. It might look a bit like this:

Through my ___________ I will achieve___________ (Specific and Measurable). I know this is (Attainable) because this goal is important to because (Relevant) and I will achieve this by (Time).

Example:

Through my determination and hard work, I will lose and maintain a weight loss of 20 pounds (specific maintain measurable 20 pounds). I know that I can achieve this because I have a strong accountability partner and the support of my doctor (Attainable). This goal is important to me because I want to dance at my daughter's wedding (Relevant and highly emotionally charged) on July 6th, 2024 (Time).

____

____

____

____

____

Exercise 4

Choose two of the daily five areas and write an action you will start tomorrow and write them below. Remember the five areas are: spirituality, health, relationships, career, knowledge.

____

____

____

____

____

Exercise 5

Write at least one big thing you learned about goals from this lesson?

____

____

____

____

____

LESSON THREE
MOVING INTO ACTION

*DREAMS INSPIRE YOU TO BUILD A LIFE BIGGER
THAN WHAT YOU HAVE NOW.
BUT DREAMS WITHOUT ACTION ARE JUST
DREAMS.*

If you want to achieve your goals and live the vision you have cast for your life and business, you need to shift from dreaming into doing. Acting means laying out a plan to achieve your goals and putting in a consistent effort to achieve them. Over time, you can make the visions of your dreams real. Big goals, dreams, and transformations are not easy, but you can do it. Why? Because you have a vision for your life, and instead of just dreaming about it, you stepped into the action and picked up this workbook. Do you realize that you have moved into the top 3% of people by doing that? According to the best research, less than 3 percent of people have written goals, and less than 1 percent review and rewrite their goals daily. You have already written your goals, and now you plan the actions needed to make them happen.

Let's take a minute and talk about Faith Vision. So often, we have Faith Vision and think that is all that is needed. Sight is a function of the eyes, while vision is a function of the heart. These two are very important to remember. The greatest gift that God gave humankind is not the gift of sight but the gift of vision. You have probably heard of the great author and wonderful entrepreneur Helen Keller, who became blind, deaf, and mute due to an illness when she was only 18 months old. She was a powerful and remarkable woman who impacted her generation, and she still influences so many today. A news reporter interviewed her about her life. Part of the conversation went like this, communicating with her through braille, he asked Miss Keller, "is there anything worse than being blind?" She paused for a moment and, in her unique way of talking, said, "What's worse than being blind is having sight without vision." What an amazing woman! This woman, who could not see physically, had more vision and accomplishments than most of her generation who had sight. Her books are still highly ready, and her poetry is terrific. Helen Keller didn't spend her time being angry and blaming God for her blindness and deafness. NO! She was able to live a full life because she had a vision in her heart.

Never Let What Your Eyes See Determine
What Your Heart Believes.

Don't Wait.

We all have been through periods of doubt, uncertainty, and questioning every move we make, but what does that ultimately lead to?

It leads to never taking that step to reach your goals that you hope and dream for in the future. Days, weeks, months go by, and you see everyone chasing after their goals, leveling up to make a difference in their life and other people, but you are still in the same place you were months ago. How does that make you feel? Let's look at a few of the traps that hold us stuck in place so that together we can move past them.

Perfection is a Trap.

The need for perfectionism or having everything perfect is a trap that keeps you from achieving your goals and dreams. Our educational system and society have told us that the real reward is only for those who get it 100% right. That idea of striving for perfection of getting an "A" on an exam, flawlessly executing a project, looking like the super fit people on the cover of most magazines is all around us. The fact is, in the world of entrepreneurship and self-transformation, perfection is more of a liability than an asset. Some things take time and experience to get right, and sometimes you need to take a leap of faith before you learn what went wrong. For example, when you first learn to ride a bike, you need to figure out balance and steering, peddling, braking, being aware of your environment, and handling different terrain. There is no way you could have learned all that by looking at a bike or reading a book about bike riding. You needed to get on the bike and feel it and test what you knew and adapt along the way.

And all these years later, you might feel confident about your bike riding skills, but would you say you are perfectly perfect in all situations? Probably not, but you still acted and started despite not being perfect.

Maybe you are going through a hard time now, and you're disheartened. You've lost your vision edge. Perhaps this is because of your surroundings. Sometimes, our environments are not the best for fostering or casting a vision. What people say to us is not always encouraging and can be very discouraging. This is the one thing that can keep us in the perfection trap—waiting for things around us to be perfect. However, we must keep our vision before us because the visions in our hearts are greater than our environments. God gave us vision so we would not live by what we only see.

Thoughts Are the Most Important,
And Words Are the Most Powerful.

Time is an Illusion.

Albert Einstein said Time is an illusion. He meant that time is our way of making sense of growing up and growing old while the world changes around us. So, if time is an illusion, finding the right time to start is probably an illusion. What I mean is there is no perfect time to start other than now. We often fail to act because we think in terms of now is not the right time. Saying things like "After the kids are grown," "once the holidays are over," "when I/We have more money saved," or "the time has passed, I'm too old and settled in my ways, or I am too out of shape." These are examples of how we use time to hold us back from acting. If one of the smartest people, Albert Einstein, said time is an illusion, then so are these time barriers to you steeping into action

Some is better than none.

Have you heard that famous story of The Tortoise and the Hare? That story is encouraging, especially when getting started or you feel like quitting,

You Don't Need to Be Big to Think Great Thoughts.
However, you Need to Think Great Thoughts
To Become Big.

Taking some action is always better than no action. Taking any step is better than taking no step. Progress is still progress and is an assurance that you have not given up. You might get frustrated with the small, slow progress and decide to give up, which is not the right thing to do. Remember, every drop of water adds up to become an ocean. Similarly, no matter how small, every action adds up to achieve success.

We all assume the moral of The Tortoise and the Hare story is that slow and steady wins the race. But the hidden lesson of the story was, it is always better to try than give up. The turtle had no chance to win against a hare, but he still chose to try. He kept taking small steps, but those small steps were moving him ahead, even if he took the time to achieve what he wanted.

Don't Overthink It.

When we need to move into action, we move from passion to logic. We forgot our "why" and started focusing on the "How." This is getting stuck in your head. That little hamster wheel of thinking takes over, and we fail to take any action. We overthink it to the degree that the opportunity is lost. So how do we break the overthinking and get into action? By focusing on the bigger picture.

Seeing the bigger picture allows us to move out of any single action that needs to be taken and into the bigger journey ahead. For example, if I asked you to walk across the room, would you have to stop and think about which foot went first, how long to make your stride, if your toe or heel should hit the ground first, should your arms swing or stay at your side or maybe the right foot and left arm should move to together and what about your head position should you look at your feet or the wall on the other side of the room? Yeah, walking across the room can be very complicated and full of lots of decisions, but did you think of any of those when I suggested you walk across the room? Most likely NO, because you had a goal of walking across the room, and you went for it. The only decision you had to make was if you were going to stand up and start. Sometimes not thinking about all the details is the best way to get into action.

Eliminate the Fear.

Fear is the big hairy monster that hides inside all of us, just looking for an opportunity to jump out and get us. As much as we would like to completely wipe it out of our lives, we can't. Fear is wired into our survival. Fear is the thing that keeps us from petting lions at the zoo. But that little monster, Fear, can also show up when there is no real danger. Unfortunately, there isn't a limit to what our brains can concoct that is potentially fearful. Some of it is legitimate, and some irrational. Either way, you can find strength and courage in faith. A great verse to call on when you are feeling afraid of a new situation is:

> *"Fear not, for I am with you; be not dismayed, for I am*
> *your God; I will strengthen you,*
> *I will help you, I will uphold you with my righteous*
> *right hand."*
> *Isaiah 41:10*

It will remind you that you are not alone, and that God is right there in the middle of it all with you. So, no matter how silly you might look, trying and failing and trying again, no matter what people might say about you and your dreams, God will uphold you. That also means your dreams, goals, and the vision for your life. Your faith is the one to push back against that little fear monster that lives in you. Another way is to ask yourself, "what's the worst that could happen?" By knowing the worst, you can prepare for it and move past it IF it happens.

Focus on the Now.

You've heard it said before—probably many times—that it's important to live in the present moment.

You also might have heard similar pieces of advice like:

"Don't get caught up in thinking about the past or the future—live in the now! Be present in your own life."

"All you have is this moment. Don't let it slip away."

All of these (possibly overused) sayings boil down to the same basic message: it's vital to live in the present moment. With so much going on in our lives and so many schedules to manage, we can get trapped in future thinking and planning and forget the only absolute control we have is in the current situation and the next best action we take. By taking a moment and becoming mindful of where you are right now, how that aligns with what you are trying to achieve, and the direction you are heading, you can do what is best. The truth is, as much as you try and plan the future or fix the past, you really can't. The only thing you can do is focus on what you need to do now, and then you do it, and you arrive at the next step and then the next. Trying to act in the now and plan for the actions for the future is like trying to walk and hop at the same time. It can't be done. Like walking, one foot moves into the future, and one foot is planted in the current step. One way to remind yourself of this when your head starts spinning is to ask yourself something like, "here, now, what do I need to do?"

A Few Benefits of Taking Action.

Everyone wants something in life. We call them dreams or goals. So, we create a vision of how we want our life to be. But, to have this vision become a reality, the most important thing required is ACTION. Action will give you what you always desire. But, to get your desired outcome, you need to act. Acting can be difficult, but it is required to move you towards your vision, and that first action has lots of benefits. Here are just a few.

Action Creates Momentum.

Each action you take will create energy, creating momentum. That momentum will move you closer and closer to what you want. The best part of all of this is that the action energy, directed towards what you want to achieve, is that it will create more momentum. And you'll start seeing results with those actions you're taking. Let's say, for instance, you start a business, and you make your first $100. Then suddenly, you make the next $100, then $1,000, and then $5,000. There was a time when making the first $100 might have seemed impossible, but once you achieve that $100, you had the momentum and the system to make a second $100 and a third and a fourth, and soon you arrived at a $1,000 and guess what happens? You now have $1000 momentum pushing you forward, not $100 momentum. That is what is so exciting about this idea of momentum working exponentially, and it's backed by science. You have heard it said, an object in motion stays in motion. Acting is the start of that motion or momentum energy.

Action Provide Feedback.

Feedback can only occur in response to an action or behavior. You can't know how good you are at something until you try. Being a good leader or successful at anything doesn't happen by luck, but from having a strong sense of self-awareness and seeking input and feedback. We can't know our ability to make good decisions unless we act, and we can't really know the impact of those actions without some form of feedback. Feedback can come in the form of customer responses, our checkbook balance, the reactions of the people around us, and our feelings. If we really want to be successful, we must be willing to act and receive positive and negative feedback and then make decisions based on that feedback. A quick note: not everything given as feedback is really feedback. You should listen to feedback that is focused on the process or actions you're taking to achieve your goals. A quick example: "You will never make it" vs. "It will be difficult to arrive where you want to go heading that direction, California is west, not north of here." The second feedback understood your goal looked at your current actions and offered corrections that supported your goal without speaking about your abilities.

Action Changes Perspective.

Another benefit of acting is perspective, like climbing up a ladder. With each step, your perspective changes. The higher you go, the more you can see and discover things you would never have seen standing on the ground. When we move into action in pursuit of our goals, we shift our perspective, and we discover new strengths, new ways of doing things, new friendships, and possibly see a bigger vision for our lives than we had before we acted. There is a saying that nothing changes until something changes, could be rewritten to; you wouldn't see the world and your place in it unless you change where you are standing. Shifting our perspective is shifting our belief systems, thinking, and sense of value. And that only happens when we act.

Action Tests Our Commitment.

One of the most significant benefits of acting and staying in action is that it tests our commitment. Everyone has had that New Year's Day moment when you declare some big, bold action. You start out strong, only to give up or fade out ten days later. This happens because the challenge of acting or staying in action becomes bigger than the goal or the vision. When you show up and act and then repeat that action repeatedly and begin to act towards your goal, you tell not only yourself but the world around you what's important. You will be tested repeatedly about your commitment to what matters in your life. Building a sense of commitment is about building a sense of purpose. And when you have a purpose, you feel fulfilled, you feel of value, you feel alive. Acting is about finding our purpose and living into it fully.

EXERCISE LESSON 3

Exercise 1

You wrote out three S.M.A.R.T goals based on your "I want" statement in the last lesson. Rewrite each of those now. Remember, only 3% of people write their goals, and lonely 1% write and review their goals daily. Do you want to be in the 99% or the 1%?

____

____

____

____

____

Exercise 2

These goals or dreams are not new. They probably have appeared on some type of list or vision board in your past. For each goal, you listed what stopped you from acting in the past?

____

____

____

____

____

Exercise 3

Now that you know the traps that stop you from acting and how to take action, and the benefits of taking action, what act, big or small, are you committing to take for each of the goals above, and which of the three benefits do you want to tap into?

____

____

____

____

____

Exercise 4

Take each of the goals listed above and use the following framework.

My goal is (exercise #1); this time, I will not allow (exercise #2) to stop me. Instead, I will (exercise #3 (action step)) so that I can (benefit (exercise #3)).

____

____

____

____

____

Exercise 5

How do you feel about your goals and your ability to achieve them? Take a moment and write those feelings below.

____

____

____

____

____

LESSON FOUR
OVERCOMING SETBACKS

WHEN YOU HAVE A SETBACK IN YOUR LIFE. YOU CAN CHOSE TO BE DISCOURAGED OR FIND THE COURAGE TO MOVE FORWARD.

How many times have you worked hard to achieve a personal goal only to find yourself feeling defeated or hopeless because your plan got knocked off track following a significant setback? The truth is everyone faces setbacks. Some are more visible to the world than the rest, but setbacks are encountered by anyone moving towards something big. The funny thing about setbacks is that they often are equal and opposite to the goal we are trying to achieve. History is filled with people and projects that had a major setback before becoming a breakthrough. For example, before any Apollo mission flew, NASA had a major setback when Gus Grissom, Ed White, and Roger Chaffee conducted a simulation on the launch pad in Florida when a fire broke out, killing all three men. The loss of life was a tragedy. And to have this setback occur on the launch pad during training could have made most turn back and say, it's not meant to be.

However, NASA and the following crew knew the vision to reach the moon was too big to give up, faced the fears and possible future failures, and pushed ahead.

So, let's accept that setbacks will happen at some point and develop some tools to handle them.

How You Think Is How You React.

The first thing we have to do is shift our thinking from "not me to why not me." If we approach life with *"it's not going to happen to me"* mindset, we will always be in reaction mode when a setback happens. However, if we approach the journey ahead with a why not me mindset, we understand that setbacks happen to everyone to some degree. Therefore, we move into proactive mode and stay focused on the vision rather than the problem. Let's take a minute and look at three possible ways to prepare for a setback.

Plan Ahead.

Know what areas or triggers could result in setbacks or failure and have a plan or alternative in place for predictable situations. Often not having enough time to follow through with the plan is a common reason for a setback. For example, you set the goal to work out every morning, and you tell yourself you're going to get up every morning at 5 am and hit the treadmill. Week one, you are 100 percent on track. Week two is a bit of a struggle; you are feeling a bit worn down, but you still hit the goal, then bang, you have a sick kid up all night, you lay down just for a quick sleep committed to getting up in 45 minutes to hit the treadmill and instead you hit the snooze and your winning streak is blown.

Setback! You feel defeated; people around you say don't beat yourself up; you had a good reason, but, in your gut, you know that your history of one missed workout leads to two, then five, then you give up altogether. How could we change this pattern and defeat the trigger of failure? Let's say on day one, you packed a gym bag and placed it in the trunk of your car just in case the morning routine got interrupted. You knew you had a plan in place to turn your lunch hour into a make-up session and stay on track. We can't plan for every setback, but let's be honest, we know the things that have knocked us off track in the past. This time let's plan how to stay committed to the bigger vision.

Strategize.

Part of planning is strategizing. The difference is when we strategize, we call in other people to help us create the plan and then execute on that plan when a setback happens. I like to think of these people as my emergency response team that has been fully trained and prepared for what needs to happen. One great tool can be your family. Maybe in the past, it was difficult to get their support, or you felt like you were going it alone, and no one cared. My experience is that they cared; they were just unaware. We can't expect others to know what we need if we don't communicate with them. So, sit down with your family or your team or maybe a group of trusted friends and explain your goal, outline the actions you're taking and the areas that you're concerned about being possible triggers for a setback. Then ASK for advice and support on successfully navigating those setbacks so you can stay on track. Help them see how much a part they are in you achieving something important and meaningful to you.

> *"Today, no leader can afford to be indifferent to the challenge of engaging others in the work of creating the future. Engagement may have been optional in the past, but it's pretty much the whole game today."*
> *Gary Hamel*

Build A Mindset of Victory, Not Victim.

When a setback or failure occurs, we can quickly jump back to the old mindset of not being good enough, always a failure, not one of the lucky few. That mindset is not only untrue, but it robs us of any chance of getting back in the game and fighting for what we want.

The biblical commandment to "love your neighbor as yourself" is well known. But we often focus on the first part of the commandment -- presumably because we take the second part for granted— the part about loving ourselves. Somehow, we have been taught that loving ourselves is selfish and being selfish is wrong. Yet, the Bible tells us differently. The love that we show others starts with the love we show ourselves.

Do you struggle with self-love because of past failures or some other perceived shortcoming? Know that you're not alone. Even the most successful people, the ones that look like they have it all together, struggle with the self-love thing.

What separates those who achieve their goals from the rest is that when a setback happens, they choose to challenge the voices (their own or others) that tell them that they are unworthy of love, success, and happiness. Instead, they offer themselves grace and understand that the setback is part of the process, not part of who they are, and get back on track. So God tells us in Hebrews 10:35 "Cast not away, therefore, your confidence, which hath a great reward." God is saying you can't give up on yourself until He gives up on you and He will never give up, so get back into that victory mindset.

Taking Action.

We have talked about preparing for a setback now, what do we do when it happens.

Get In Motion and Use Momentum.

When a setback happens, the first thing we want to do is get in motion. Sitting with a plan in hand and not executing is like sitting in the sun with an ice cream cone and not taking a lick—a complete waste of a plan and ice cream. So often, we want to get wrapped up in a feeling of defeat and fear. Moving into action takes us out of the feelings and into the plan. I am not saying don't feel, but as John Maxwell says, "if it goes on for more than twenty-four hours, it turns into a pity party, and no one wants to be part of that." Before you started, you planed for a setback, and you talked to friends and family about what you would need when it occurred. So, step into that plan and act, and the thing about action is that one action leads to another and then to another, and soon you have built the momentum needed to move past the setback and the emotion of failure and back into a feeling of excitement about pursuing your purpose.

Focus On What You Can Control.

The second thing is to focus on what you can control and not what you can't. Your own opinions, attitudes, aspirations, dreams, desires, and goals are within your control. We control how we spend our time, what books we consume, how productive we are, what we eat, the number of hours we choose to sleep, and who we choose to spend time with.

Outside our control sits everything else: life's events unfolded, the weather, the economy, other people…

Trying to control or change what isn't within your control will only drain your energy and leave you in torment. Instead, you can control how you perceive a situation, how you react to it, and how you respond.

The reality is this: Even though you might not like the situation you are in, you can choose to accept it. Once you learn to accept what is and then focus on what you can control, you win. 2020 was a perfect example. COVID and its impact on your business, family, and economy were not in your control; however, how you chose to respond and adapt was. Many people decided to use the time to grow family relationships, develop a business, write a book, and others sat on the sideline talking about everything out of their control and waiting for someone to fix it.

When a setback happens, focus on what you can control, even if it is just your attitude.

Have Faith and Act Accordingly.

Thirdly, having faith should not be the last resort but a first response. When setbacks happen, think of Philippians 1:6 "God didn't bring you this far to leave you." If you're a person of faith, you need to place faith not as an insurance but as an assurance. The word assurance means a promise or guarantee. You have been told you are not alone and that vision you have for your life is given to you by God. You need to take that promise, shift that mindset, pull out that plan, and get into action.

How to Learn from a Setback.

If setbacks are to become setups for success, we need to be able to glean learning from that setback. So, let's talk about how to learn from a setback.

Seek Feedback.

Often, what we want to do after a failure or a setback is to ask others for feedback. The fear of drawing attention to what happened can feel like opening an old wound. But to gain perspective on what happened, we often need the perspective of others. I mean those that can add insight and value to your plan. Almost as important as asking for feedback is the state of mind you're in when receiving it. Receiving input isn't always easy, especially if you don't like or agree with it. Your mindset is everything when it comes to receiving feedback. Your response when getting feedback in the past may have been to step into denial or defensiveness. That will not serve you if you intend to grow. Instead, you should try to understand the situation from the perspective of the feedback provider. Understand that they are most likely giving that feedback with positive intent if you show you are open to listening with an open mind. Remind yourself that constructive feedback isn't personal. It focuses on the system or process against the desired outcome.

Remove the Ego and See the Situation.

Let's talk about EGO for a second. The ego is all about self-condemnation and self-criticism, or the criticism and condemnation of others. It makes you unsafe.

Ego does not cause people to want to work with you, and it does not cause people to want to trust or refer you. It only drives people to want to stay away from you.

Ego comes in many disguises. You may not think you have an ego, but see if you recognize any of these ego masks:

- The Blame Ego. Loves to play the blame game for its lack of results. This ego says it's their fault!

- The Know-it-all Ego says. I already know all this stuff.

- The Fearful Ego loves to speak fear. What if I say the wrong thing? What if I do the wrong thing?

- There's the Comfort Zone Ego. Okay, we are good right where we are! We are happy with the things we have.

- Self-Righteous Ego. Oh, my goodness! I never talk like that. I thought you were a Godly person. Oh, you don't need to be wearing clothes like that. Always have more and always better.

- The Judgmental Ego is constantly judging everybody else. They are not that great! Who do they think they are?

- The People-Pleasing Ego tries to cover up its insecurities by constantly trying to keep everybody happy. Therefore, these people sacrifice themselves to help others.

- Jealous Ego is envious in a bad way of other people's success.

- Fake Ego puts on a different face with every group they are around. They can never be themselves because they have to hide their true personality.

- The Other People's Opinion Ego. These folks always care more about other's opinions than what they truly want.

It's time to confront your ego and its many disguises. Take off that disguise and throw it out the window. Ego's will never do anything for you but keep you broke and broken-hearted.

To move forward, you must first understand that failure, or a setback is external, not internal. It's about the process, not the person. If you look at the situation objectively, you are more likely to see ways that you can improve both as a person and the process.

Reset and Get Back on Track.

We have taken the time to get feedback. We have listened with open heart and mind. Now what?

We need to reset and get back on track. Here is a simple tool to RE-SET. The RESET framework works like this:

- Reflect on your past and decide your future – Reflect without judgment or blame.

- Evaluate your priorities to pursue the right goals – Check in to see if the goal still supports the vision and that it is in alignment with your strength and passion.

- Simplify instead of over complicate – Break down the process to the most straightforward short steps and start there.

- Establish a plan to achieve better results in less time – Check the plan and make sure that you have a clear objective and you're not just going through the motions.

- Time Block actions that fast-track extraordinary results – set a deadline to get back in action and reset the timeline for the goal.

Don't give up. Get clear on how far you've come and where you want to be. Don't let the setback become your story. Instead, let your comeback be your story.

EXERCISES FOR LESSON 4

Exercise 1

Last week you rewrote your goals using the format.

My goal (goal) this time I will not allow(obstacle/excuse) to stop me; instead, I will (action step) so that I can experience (benefit). Let's take a moment and rewrite those statements below as we will be using them in the following exercises:

____

____

____

____

____

Exercise 2

Look at each of the goals you listed and write a possible setback/ failure that could occur.

____

____

____

____

____

Exercise 3

For each possible setback, take turns in your groups to strategize a way to get back on track or stay on track. Make sure that the strategy is focused on the goal.

Write two strategies for each goal below.

____

____

____

____

Exercise 4

Take each of the goals listed in exercise #1 and rewrite it using the following format.

My goal (goal) this time I will not allow(obstacle/excuse) to stop me; instead, I will (action step) so that I can experience (benefit). Adding the one strategy, you will use to overcome a setback.

____

____

____

____

____

Exercise 5

You're at the halfway point in the Start with Vision Study Guide. Congratulations! Take a moment and write down a few Aha moments you have had. What's an Aha moment? It is a point in your life when an important insight, choice, or decision is made.

____

____

____

____

____

CHAPTER FIVE
JUMPING THE GAPS

GOD WAITS IN THE GAPS.

What Are "Gaps"?

If you have dreams, goals, or aspirations, you will need to grow to achieve them. But if you're like I was—and if you're like most people—you have one or more mistaken beliefs that create a gap that keeps you from growing and reaching your potential.

These mistaken beliefs are what John C Maxwell calls Growth Gap Traps in his book *The 15 Invaluable Laws.* Gaps can be tricky things, they can lead to excuses and keep you from reaching your goals. But the good news is, once you know about Growth Gaps, you can prepare strategies to help you bridge the gaps.

What Are the Types of Growth Gaps?

For now, I am going to only provide a brief overview of the eight gaps identified in *The 15 Invaluable Laws of Growth* under the Law of Intentionality. If you want to know more, I encourage you to get a copy of the book; it's amazing.

- The Assumption Gap - "I assume I will automatically grow."

- The Knowledge Gap - "I don't know how to grow."

- The Timing Gap – "It's not the right time to begin."

- The Mistake Gap – "I'm afraid of making mistakes."

- The Perfection Gap – "I have to find the best way before I start."

- The Inspiration Gap – "I don't feel like doing it."

- The Comparison Gap – "Others are better than I am."

- The Expectation Gap – "I thought it would be easier than this."

How often have you found yourself saying something that sounds like one of the above? But the truth is, it does not matter what level of personal development we have achieved when we face something new and face one or more of these Gaps. Oh, and once we think we have crossed over that gap, it pops back up. So, when we choose to become intentional about carrying out the vision we have for our life, we have to become intentional about remaining aware of the Growth Gaps and, from the start, building strategies to overcome these gaps.

How To Overcome The Growth Gaps?

Let me first say that one of the greatest gaps in the world is the difference between knowing and doing. As Oprah is famous for saying, "now that you know better, your expected to do better."

Doing better is done by becoming intentional. This Law of Intentionality is the first law of the fifteen and is where the Growth Gaps are found. The Law of Intentionality is a perfect place to start personal growth because it empowers us to make trans-formative intentional decisions that can shift our lives and those around us.

The Law of Intentionality also reminds me of a verse in the Bible that says:

"That I have set before you life and death, blessing and cursing that both thou and thy seed may live." (Deuteronomy 30:19) Paraphrasing a bit, I would say… that both thou and thy vision may grow.

If you have doubted your ability to make a change in your life. This verse speaks directly to the power of your choices. You are given this ability by your choices for life over death, blessings over hardship, growth over decay. This power of choice applies to every area of life, faith, and personal development. To be clear, a choice is an intentional action.

Personal Growth is a choice and must be done on purpose, not by accident. It needs to be planned out - like developing a personal curriculum for lifelong learning and development.

Growth is not an automatic process.

I want to look at a simple way to start to overcome each of these gaps.

- ***The Assumption Gap*** - "I assume I will automatically grow."

  - ▸ How to overcome it? - Don't assume anything; make it your intention to grow.

- ***The Knowledge Gap*** - "I don't know how to grow."

  - ▸ How to overcome it? - Stop making excuses and decide to grow, even if you don't know- how.

- ***The Timing Gap*** – "It's not the right time to begin."

  - ▸ How to Overcome it? – The reality is, there is never a more "right" time to begin than now.

- ***The Mistake Gap*** – "I'm afraid of making mistakes."

  - ▸ How to Overcome it? - Get over your fear of making mistakes, accept that making them is an essential part of your growth.

- ***The Perfection Gap*** – "I have to find the best way before I start."

  - ▸ How to overcome it? – Know that starting is the only way to find the best way. Even the experts had to start somewhere.

- ***The Inspiration Gap*** – "I don't feel like doing it."

> How to overcome it? – Do it anyway, even if you don't feel like it; acting upon it will eventually inspire you to keep on doing it.

- ***The Comparison Gap*** – "Others are better than I am."

  > How to overcome it? – Learn from others who are better than you. Your greatest competition isn't them, and it has always been you and only you.

- ***The Expectation Gap*** – "I thought it would be easier than this."

  > How to overcome it? – Know that there is no easy road to any place worth going. If you find yourself face to face with adversity, then you know you are in the right place.

In summary...

- Growth happens by intentional actions, and when you identify your visions, goals, and habits that are necessary for your intentional living, it becomes obvious that improving our life does not come automatically. Instead, it comes by understanding what you want and then implementing them in your life.

- Failure is a natural and necessary part of life, and the faster we learn that, the faster we find ourselves in a happier state of mind and blazing down the road to the kind of success we want to achieve for our lives.

- Gaining awareness around the gaps you have is one of the quickest ways to figure out how to do things as effectively and efficiently as possible, meet your goals, and make those dreams happen.

Fueling Up to Jumping the Gaps.

Knowing the Growth Gaps and how to overcome them is the beginning. But knowing a problem and knowing the solution can often be the most frustrating thing in the world. It's like climbing in a car with no gas. You know where you are and where you want to go, but you don't have the fuel to get there. So, let's take a minute and brainstorm a few fuel sources for you to be able to use to cross those gaps.

- People:

You're not alone so that you can find help. There's no need to feel ashamed for asking for help. Whether you choose to rely on a loved one, a stranger, a mentor, or a friend, there are people who want to help you succeed. Asking for help is only one side of the coin. On the other side of the coin, you have to be open and willing to accept support. People who come to your aid truly do care about you. Be open to receiving help when you need it.

Your journey and vision are your own, but that does not mean you can't learn from other people's experiences. Remember when you were little and wanted to learn to ride a bike? You didn't start by learning how to build a bike. Instead, you trusted someone to show you the appropriate bike for you to begin with, and they probably made sure you had a level surface to start learning on. You still had to find your own balance, but you had someone, or maybe a few someones helping you get started and removing obstacles to your success. As you move through this journey towards your vision, you will need to add people and sometimes remove people from your journey.

- Tools:

We are in a time of instant access to tools. We have tools all around us, books, webinars, YouTube, social media, Podcasts. No matter where you are in the world, no matter what level of education or income, you have equal access to the tools you need to cover the gaps and achieve your vision. So when you build your growth plan, schedule intentional tool time. Find a book, a webinar, podcast somethings, and invest time into learning and growing, and equipping yourself to manage the gaps that will appear as you make this journey.

A quick warning, don't let yourself slip into a rabbit hole of watching endless videos and not taking action. Remember, the greatest gap is the gap between knowing and doing. Use the 80/20 rule, 80% of the time doing and 20% learning how.

- Self:

You are fully equipped. If He called you, He equipped you. Unfortunately, many of us feel unworthy of our vision calling us to do. You're not alone when we feel insufficient for whatever your vision has called you to do. The Bible gives us numerous examples of everyday people who doubted their abilities to carry out the vision they had. At the beginning of Exodus, Moses is called to a daunting task. God hands him the vision of how Moses will deliver the Israelites from Egypt with the burning bush.

When Moses walks away from the encounter with God, he doesn't respond with a lot of enthusiasm. You don't see him rushing down the mountain yelling. "I got it, I can do it, let's go." Instead, we see him filled with questions and doubts, saying things like "Who am I that I should go to Pharaoh and bring the children of Israel out of Egypt" (Exodus. 3:11)? Your Moses size doubts might sound more like "who am I to go after that big client" or "that big dream." Remember Moses had doubts but was equipped with what he needed when he needed to carry out the vision.

> *"God is able to make all grace abound to you, so that*
> *having all sufficiency in all things at all times, you may*
> *abound in every good work"*
> *(2 Cor. 9:8)*

If you have been given a vision for your life, you will be given what it takes to carry it through. He will give us the grace and the tools needed to accomplish the vision. Maybe not perfectly—in fact, certainly not—but all he asks is our service, leaving the outcome to him.

EXERCISES FOR LESSON 5

Exercise 1

Let's take a moment and update our goals, yep, one more time. Using the following format

I will achieve my goal _______________(goal) this time because I will not allow__________(obstacle/excuse) to stop me. Instead, I will__________ (action step) so that I can experience _______________ (benefit of the goal). I accept that gaps of__________ & ___________ are part of the growth process. (Name two possible gaps you see right now).

____

____

____

____

____

Exercise 2

Look at each of the goals you listed above and the possible gaps you identified, and write a brief statement of how in the past these gaps showed up in your life?

____

____

____

____

____

Exercise 3

For each of the gaps, you listed above, take turns in your groups to strategize possible ways to use the tools you identified to overcome the gaps. Make sure that the strategy is focused on intentional action leading to the goal.

Write two tool use strategies for each goal below

____

____

____

____

____

Exercise 4

Take each of the goals listed in exercise #1 and rewrite it using the following format.

I will achieve my goal_____________ (goal) this time because I will not allow_________(obstacle/excuse) to stop me. Instead, I will_____________(action step) so that I can experience_______________ (benefit of the goal). I accept that the gap_______________ (pick one) is a natural part of the growth process and will use the following tool in the following way to grow through the gap.

Goal 1.

____

____

____

____

____

Goal 2.

____

____

____

____

Goal 3.

____

____

____

____

____

Exercise 5

Facilitator led.

Start by taking a few deep breaths. (Play soft classical music if you want) then close your eyes and silently make the following affirmation, "I am fully resourced to achieve my vision." Now repeat, "I am fully resourced to achieve my vision," but this time you're your hands placed over your heart, give a moment to let this affirmation settle in, then repeat one more time "I am fully resourced to achieve my vision" with your hands still over their heart. Allow yourself to feel that sense of having all the tools necessary to achieve your dreams. It can be easy to accept that we are fully resourced intellectually, but to trust, we are at a different level of power. This exercise helps with that deeper connection. At the end of the exercise, I encourage you to return to this exercise anytime they feel overwhelmed or in doubt.

LESSON SIX
BUILDING SYSTEMS FOR SUCCESS

THE STUDENT HAS GOALS.
THE MASTER HAS SYSTEMS TO REACH THEM.

Your growth plan is a strategy to become the best version of yourself. It includes your goals and how to achieve them, skills to master, and habits to develop, along with the resources you will need to reach success. None of this would happen without a system. When you develop System Thinking, it allows you to take control of your life and gives you the ability to reduce it to a manageable set of inputs and outputs and establish some predictability. A haphazard collection of tools, habits, and methods is not the same as a purposeful system. Let's look at what a system is.

What Is A "System?"

- A system needs to be designed to accomplish a focused purpose. A good system does not exist for itself. It serves a purpose. To build a good system, start with a clearly defined purpose.

We often try and build our success by working with various tools, methods, and habits picked up at different times from different sources and teachers. The problem is since our tools aren't built or bought with a unifying goal in mind, they often create system self-sabotage. We may have become so comfortable with the mix-matched tools that we don't see the conflict; we say things like, "it gets the job done what's the problem." The problem is lost time and energy.

When you start to build a system, you have to avoid component conflict by creating a system with a defined purpose. The purpose will give you guidelines for when and how the system should function.

A system is designed to create efficiencies, not complexity.

When you design a system to accomplish one purpose, all the components need to be planned and put in place to create efficiencies. In addition, systems are supposed to reduce conflict (which reduces resource use) because everything moves toward a single purpose.

Over time we often do things in a particular way for no good reason, the "well, that's the way we always have done it" syndrome. When we audit or review our methods, we might see a lot of overlap, unnecessary work, or back-and-forth action that can be eliminated. To build a good system, question every component and only keep the necessary ones. That kind of scrutiny minimizes waste, minimizes the resources needed, and maximizes the output of each use of the system.

- A system is designed with all the elements needed to accomplish the purpose.

How often have you attempted to do a task—only to find you don't have all the information or tools you need?

It's incredibly frustrating and unproductive to stop and search for the necessary stuff. Often this frustration and delay lead to you putting the task off, again. Any task you have to do repeatedly, even if it's only annually, can benefit from a system. The system can be simple, but it must contain all the information and tools needed to accomplish its purpose. If it doesn't, it's not a system; it's a half-built system, and it's not usable.

- A system is repeatable and teachable.

If systems are consistent, they repeat in much the same way every time; that repetition makes it easy for you to teach someone else how to use the system. When you can teach something, you can delegate it, outsource it, or, at the very least, streamline it, so it takes up less of your time.

When you design, any system, remember your goal is to be able to teach it. You know how to do each step, but someone learning the system will need an explanation of each step and the why behind that step. So, write it that way from the start.

- A system leads to a predictable outcome.

A good system needs to be developed to provide two kinds of predictability. First, a system enables you to predict the tools and resources required for any task or goal to be accomplished by the system. Knowing how long a specific task will take, how many resources you will need, how often it must be done builds predictable resource assignment. Since a system allows you to do a task in the same way, every time, you can predict almost everything about the process. How much it will take to start and what it will produce when completed.

Second, a system provides some predictability for the entire area the system covers. Knowing what is required in one area of your life helps you better build predictability in other areas. Third, since a system is used the same way every time, you can start capturing data for the area.

Finding patterns is key to future prediction. Knowing what got you to one level of success will help you understand what to invest in to take you to the next level.

- A system is always in change.

Systems are never perfect. Our needs change: the obstacles we need to overcome or the goals we want to accomplish change. Systems can never be static. You will need to build a regular review period into you every system and be ready to make adjustments. Beware of system-tweaking as a means of procrastination; if system-tweaking becomes a way to avoid important tasks, set limits on yourself.

Schedule a regular time (monthly, quarterly, or at the end of a productive week) for rebuilding, testing, and adjusting systems.

The Resources You Need to Build Any System.

When you build systems, you are really doing "resource management." Resource management is the process of pre-planning, scheduling, and allocating your current and future resources to maximize efficiency for the desired outcome at the lowest cost. We all have the same resources to build our systems, Time, Energy, Attention, and Money (TEAM). By building systems to manage your T.E.A.M., you can live a more fulfilled, more successful life, knowing your most precious resources are being spent mindfully.

Don't tell me where your priorities are.
Show me where you spend your resources, and I'll tell
you what they are.

Resource #1

Time

Time is the most precious and most limited resource we have. And we have no idea how much of it we have left. Still, we spend a lot of it mindlessly. We get lost checking our phone, scrolling through cat videos, or watching an entire season on Netflix, mindlessly giving away chunks of time.

Have you ever said, "I would like to (blank), but I just don't have the time"?

It's time (no pun intended!) to change the language you use. It's time to take control of what you spend your time doing and make it a conscious decision about the value of this limited resource.

This is not about scheduling every minute of your day to do something productive. Rest and time off are great and should be highly valued. It's about knowing what you spend your time doing and deciding if this aligns with your goals, values, and priorities. Before you start making changes to your schedule, you need to have a clear picture of where you are spending your Time Resource. I mean really spending our time. Not what we think or wish we spent our time doing! One way to do this is to do a time audit. A time audit is a process you do over one, or preferably a few, days where you write down everything you spend your time doing. It needs to be detailed. If it's just a general overview, it's not actually going to tell you anything! Remember to be honest. You can now make the changes you need with the information in hand.

Resource #2

Energy

We have two types of energy that we need to manage. Physical energy and mental energy. In contrast to time, we can create more energy – become more energetic – but only up to a point.

You can train yourself to work out longer or to be able to focus for longer periods, but you can only improve so much. There is a point that exercising more will not give you more energy. And a point where all the mental exercises in the world will not give you more mental energy.

But many of us have a long way to go before finding our limits! So look at where your energy is going and question if it is worth it or if there's a way to get the same result using less energy. Trying to keep going until we drop is not a sign that we're important. It's a sign that we need to take care of ourselves.

Resource #3

Attention

In today's world, everything and everyone seems to fight for your attention, from the kids needing lunch, to the spouse who can't find their glasses, to social media that keeps sending you alerts about what you will miss if you don't log in now. Yet, our attention often doesn't make the list when we consider our resources. This is because we think time and attention are the same things. But focusing our attention is not the same as spending our time or using our energy on a task.

For example, we can spend our time and energy making sure we have a great family meal, but if we spend the whole meal with our attention on our phone or worrying about work, will it matter? Attention management is about mindfulness. Mindfulness is all about paying attention to what you are doing to what is important to you. It's about becoming a student of your thoughts and actions. Mindfulness can be defined as the moment-to-moment awareness of your experience and actions. Attention is more than just how much time we spend doing something; it's also about how we do something.

How You Do Anything is How You Do Everything.
Mindful Attention Changes Everything.

Resource #4

Money

Money is not a limited resource because you can somehow make more when you need to. However, to get more, you will need to use a combination of all your resources. For example, you trade time, energy, and attention for more money.

But money can also be used the other way around! It can be used to buy yourself more time and energy. So, for example, you can hire someone to clean the house and mow the lawn, giving you both time and energy to focus on something more aligned with your goals and vision.

As you develop systems, you must ask yourself, "would it be more cost-effective to earn money to pay for someone to do this instead of doing it yourself?

The starting point for learning how to maximize any resource is to audit it. Go through your bank and credit card statements from the last couple of months and do an audit. What are you spending your money on?

Could you change your spending, so it goes more towards your priorities? Could setting a budget help you find a way to create more time or more energy?

Remember your TEAM, makes up who we are and who we're becoming. If you could look at money differently, how would things shift for you? Instead of thinking of money as something to have, think of it as a resource to use to create the life you want. Money is not good or evil. It is just a resource to be used.

Show me where you spend your money,
and I'll tell you what you value most.

To build great systems, you need to become aware of your resources and how you are currently using them. Then decide on how to apply your resource to your goals most effectively.

If anything is ever going to change, you need to make managing your TEAM a priority.

If You Are Ready For A Change.

- Do at *time* audit.
- Consider if you are spending your *energy* on the right things.
- Be mindful of what your *attention* is on.
- Look at your statements to see where you're spending your *money*.

EXERCISES FOR LESSON 6

Exercise 1

In the last lesson, you rewrote your goals in the following format:

I will achieve my goal____________(goal). I will not allow_____________ (obstacle/excuse) to stop me. Instead, I will_____________ (action step) so that I can experience (benefit of the goal). I accept that the gap _____________(pick one) is a natural part of the growth process and will use the following tool to grow through the gap_________________ (add one resource you identified in your group).

Now take a moment, rewrite each goal, and identify the top resource you feel will be required. Now update your goal using the following format.

I will achieve my goal____________ (goal). I will not allow_____________ (obstacle/excuse) to stop me. Instead, I will __________ (action step) so that I can experience the_______________ (benefit of the goal). I also accept that the gap _____________ (pick one) is a natural part of the growth process and will use the following tool to grow through the gap______________ (add one tool you identified). I will also commit the required resource _________________ (the one you feel it will take) to achieve this goal.

____

____

____

____

____

Exercise 2

Look at each of the goals you listed above and the resource you identified as needed to achieve that goal. Now do a quick audit of how you used that resource over the past week and record the results below. For example, if you need to access your bank account online, do so, if you want to review your calendar, do so, if you are brave enough to check your "screen time," do so.

1. My audit of_______(name the resource) showed me…..

2. My audit of_______(name the resource) showed me…..

3. My audit of_______(name the resource) showed me…..

____

____

____

____

____

Exercise 3

Based on your audit results, design a system using the six elements of a system you learned in this lesson to now maximize that resource for the use of achieving your goal.

Use the following format for each resource.

Goal 1.

The resource most needed:

System Statement:

To maximize my resource of _______________ (name the resource) towards the achievement of my goal, I have designed and will use the following system:

____

____

____

____

____

Exercise 4

Homework

Complete the remaining two goals from exercise 3.

Goal 2.

The resource most needed:

System Statement:

To maximize my resource of ______________ (name the resource) towards the achievement of my goal, I have designed and will use the following system:

____

____

____

____

____

Goal 3.

The resource most needed:

System Statement:

To maximize my resource of ______________ (name the resource) towards the achievement of my goal, I have designed and will use the following system:

____

____

____

____

____

Exercise 5

Take a moment and look over your notes and the completed exercises and write three things you have learned about yourself and your goals.

____

____

____

____

____

CHAPTER 7
TAKING INVENTORY

Taking inventory is to take a deliberate pause and reflect and review. Think about it like this — what happens if a big business forgets (or refuses) to take inventory of their items? They'll likely crumble. They might be going through the motions, making sales, and attending to their storefront, but if they aren't periodically checking in on things behind the scenes, then, well, they'll fall apart. The same can be applied to taking a personal inventory.

If your daily grind has become familiar, if you're feeling unrest but can't put your finger on it, if you're stuck in your growth, then it's time to take a step back and take inventor.

What to Take Inventory of.

A great place to start is with your T.E.A.M. and your systems. In the last lesson, you identified the resources you would need and the systems to which you would apply those resources. But how would you know if you really had those tools and resources without taking inventory?

Anyone who has ever worked in retail knows you're always taking inventor at some level. Sometimes it happens on a micro-level, like when you take a detailed yearly count of every item by color, size, style, condition, cost, and value. And sometimes, it happens at a macro or large- scale level by just eyeballing to see if what you have on hand can meet the short-term needs.

We will talk more about taking a general inventory for now.

The Purpose of Taking Inventory.

As we discussed in the lesson on systems, every action we take should have a clearly defined process and purpose. So, what is the purpose of taking inventory? First, let's talk about three purposes of taking inventory.

Taking Inventory Provides Perspective.

One of the benefits of taking inventory is perspective. When you stop to look at the parts and the whole, it gives you a better sense of where you are in the bigger picture. The merry- go-round of life constantly accelerates, 'til we hit a wall and collapse the retirement home. Just like business owners do of their products, taking a regular inventory of your lives is mandatory. It helps you answer questions about the directions and paths your life is taking. Are we growing or declining in character development … in spiritual maturity? Are we moving toward our goals, or do obstacles hinder our progress? Are we striving for the right goals? Is our relationship with God growing? What changes do we need to make to move ahead more effectively? What strategies, if any, have we been using? And more importantly, are these strategies working to achieve the right goals? Trying to answer these questions while in the process would be like changing a tire while driving down the highway. You have to take an intentional time out and pull away from the hour-to-hour day-to-day of what you are doing and get a little perspective.

Taking Inventory Points Out Priorities.

Taking inventory helps us figure out what is our real priority. We can talk about our priorities, but we will never really know until we stop and take inventory of our resource management. For example, how would you know if the goal you set to save 10% of your income was happening unless you stopped to a look at your bank account? In *Start with Vision: You don't have to be perfect to be amazing;* you were introduced to S.M.A.R.T. goal setting in the chapter on "Goals". Do you remember what the M stood for? Measurable.

These things that are a priority in our growth should be measurable. If they are not, then it's time to reassess if they are still a priority or if some other life events has caused us to make a shift. But, on the other hand, if the goal is still a priority, then taking inventory allows us to check our resources and systems and make the adjustments to get back on track.

Taking Inventory Creates Predictability.

Another benefit of taking inventory is it allows us to predict what T.E.A.M. resources we will need in the future. In short, if we know what it took to get us where we are at, we will be able to predict what it will require to take us to the next level. All too often, we start out thinking, "I got this," only to end up at the halfway point without the Time, Energy, Attention, or Money to keep going? And when this happens, we either stop and wait, or give up. By taking inventory at the start and along the way, you will know what's in the tank and fuel up before you run out and get stuck on the side of the road.

Taking Inventory Allows Time for Praise.

When we stop and see all that we have done, how far we have come, the impact we are making, and the lives we are changing, giving praise seems like a natural thing to do. Yet, we struggle with it sometimes.

Here are three ways praise will help you breakthrough and go to the next level.

Praise brings strength - Praise and strength are synonymous. Praise brings strength into your life: spiritual strength, mental strength, emotional strength, and even physical strength.

Praise silences the enemy – The enemy is often the fear, stress, guilt, shame, etc., trying to drive our thinking and actions. Praising your journey silences the fears and doubts. God wants to silence those voices so you can clearly hear His voice and the vision He has for your life.

Praise activates answers - If the circumstances are overwhelming and you feel lost on what to do next, praise. When you take time to see that you have chosen achievement over affirmation, excellence over acceptability, personal growth over immediate pleasure, future potential over financial gain, narrow focus over scattered interests, and significance over security, you realize that you have been fully resourced. God has not brought you this far without preparing the tools and resources you need to finish the journey.

Let every opposition strengthen you rather than stop you.

What exactly does a personal inventory entail? It all boils down to honesty—honesty with yourself. During this time of honest reflection, you might consider some of the following questions:

- What is your current life position? Do you think you are in a good place, or are you not where you had hoped to be?

- What do you have going for you right now? What is in your "plus" column? Think about relationships, friends, work, hobbies that give you satisfaction—anything.

- What do you lack? What would you put in your "minus" column?

- What are some of your dreams and goals? What is standing between you and meeting those goals?

- What are some of the personal or moral failings that have led you to experience trouble, or that have kept you from reaching your goals? This is the hardest one to answer, but it is critically important.

- How have your habits affected you and the people around you?

- What are some traits or characteristics that strengthen you?

- To make progress in your life—you have to be honest about who you are and where you stand. That is not always a pleasant experience, but it is a necessary one—and it may help point you down the road to further recovery.

How to Take Inventory.

3 Ways to take inventory.

The way you take inventory will depend on two things. First, the goal and second system you are designing to achieve that goal. If the goal and system were built around the actions and results of you alone, then it becomes a personal accountability review process; if it includes others, then it requires gathering as a team and reflecting and reviewing.

Either way, you can take inventory by looking at three areas.

1. The Growth – how far you have Grown from where you started when you started.

2. The Gap – how much you have learned or closed the gaps.

3. The Goal – how close you are to achieving the goal.

No matter what you measure.

- Don't look only at the failures.

- Use facts, not feelings, to measure.

- Be honest.

- Don't blame.

- Seek to learn.

- Offer grace and room for growth.

The Benefits of Taking Inventory.

If actions are to be intentional, they should also have a benefit or, in business-speak an R.O.I. (Return on Investment).

The R.O.I. on taking inventory is.

- It gives time to learn – you get to learn what's working, what's not working, what team members' strengths are, and where you need to invest more resources.

- It gives you time to recharge – when we take intentional time to discount from the day- to-day operations of building a business and transforming our lives and reflect, you get a chance to recharge. Not only your energy but your vision.

- It gives you time to plan and adjust – taking time out to plan vs. being in 24/7 reaction mode is one of the greatest energy boosts you can give yourself.

- It gives a chance to get to know YOU. *To Thine Own Self Be True.* The power of this statement lies in the fact that it has a double meaning. The first is meant to instill an essential ingredient of success: understanding the importance of "rigorous honesty." Before you can be honest with anyone, you first have to be honest with yourself. The second is an encouragement to live from the inside out, to be who you are, not who other people expect you to be.

Taking personal inventory provides insight into who you are; it offers you encouragement as you see the areas in which you have grown, and it challenges you with new areas for growth and development to become the person you were called to be.

EXERCISES LESSON 7

Exercise 1

You currently have your goals written in the following format from the last lesson:

To will achieve my goal___________ (goal). I will not allow_______________ (obstacle/excuse) to stop me. Instead, I will ___________ (action step) so that I can experience the ___________ (benefit of the goal). I also accept that the gap_____________ (pick one) is a natural part of the growth process and will use the following tool to grow through the gap_______________ (add one tool you identified). I will also commit the required resource _______________ (the one you feel it will take) to achieve this goal.

Rewrite them below by adding the following: and I will pause and take inventory of to make sure I have what it takes.

____

____

____

____

____

Exercise 2

It might seem early to start taking inventory but knowing what you have at hand will better prepare you for the road ahead. "To see where you are going, you have to know where you are at." So, take a moment and answer these questions:

What do you have going for you right now?

____

____

____

____

____

What is in your "plus" column?

____

____

____

____

What do you lack?

____

____

____

____

What would you put in your "minus" column?

____

____

____

____

Exercise 3

How will you measure a change of those things you listed in the minus column?

(By The Growth, The Gap, The Goal). Write a few ideas of how you will measure change.

____

____

____

____

Exercise 4

Time for praise! Take a moment and offer praise to yourself.

"God bestowed dignity upon us when he created us in his image," (Gen. 1:26-27). It is His image in us that gives us value—value that exists apart from our appearance, life experience, or contribution to society. Therefore, in acknowledging and praising the person you are, you praise the image of God that lives in you.

Write your response below using the following format. (Your Name) I want to acknowledge and praise you for….

____

____

____

____

____

The writer of Hebrews tells us, "Do not throw away your confidence; it will be richly rewarded. You need to persevere (need patience) so that when you have done the will of God, you will receive what he has promised". (Hebrews 10;35-36) People who have long patience will always win.

CHAPTER EIGHT
BUILDING CONNECTIONS

*FOR THE PERSON WHO AIMS TO MAKE A
DIFFERENCE,
COMMUNICATION IS
PARAMOUNT. AND
COMMUNICATION STARTS
WITH CONNECTIONS.*

Truly connecting with others is a skill and quality that seems to be fading in our world. With social media being as popular and widely used as it is, and with everyone wanting to push their thoughts and feelings, we seem to have replaced connecting with communicating. So often we put communicating and connecting in the same category; however, they are actually very different. Communicating to people is simple and can be done by anyone. Connecting with people is more challenging and comes from the heart. Connecting is intentional. It is about us moving toward an individual, their experiences, and their needs. It is about putting yourself in that other person's life, getting out of your world, and getting into theirs. The most successful people are the ones that connect with individuals; they focus interactions with others beyond just communicating. Although communicating can be effective, nothing is as effective as a genuine connection with another human being.

Definition of communicating: To convey knowledge of or information about.

Definition of connecting: To place or establish a relationship.

The Value of Connections.

- Connections can lead to new opportunities

You've heard it before: it's all about who you know. But what does that mean?

Making connections leads to conversations, and conversations lead to opportunities. Beyond making connections, it's vital to spend time nurturing connections as they can come in handy in unexpected ways down the road. Connections are the most important way to advance in your vision.

- Connections can lead to new perspectives

Your connections can be an excellent source of new perspectives and ideas. It's easy to get caught up in the day-to-day of your professional realm and end up in a rut. You can gain insights that only come from viewing a situation with fresh eyes by talking to others. Asking for opinions from contacts you trust or admire can help you see things in a new light and overcome roadblocks that you might not have known how to circumvent otherwise.

- Connections can grow confidence

By continually putting yourself out there and meeting new people, you're effectively stepping outside your comfort zone and building invaluable social skills and self-confidence that you can take with you anywhere. The more you connect, the more you'll grow and learn how to make lasting connections.

- Connections increase passion

Ever feel like your creative juices are running dry? Or maybe your passion for life and your business are? Before beating yourself up about losing your drive, try looking at what might be missing from your life and make your friend list your starting point.

Connecting with friends and professional peers is a great way to re-ignite fizzling interests and creativity. Quality time with creative and like-minded people can be just the thing to motivate and inspire you find that lost passion.

- Connections keep you healthy.

The link between connections and good mental health are numerous. A few of the proven links include lower rates of anxiety and depression, higher self-esteem, greater empathy, and more trusting and cooperative relationships. Strong, healthy connections can also help to strengthen your immune system, help you recover from disease, and may even lengthen your life.

With so many great reasons to grow connections, the obvious question is how?

How to Build Connections.

Moving from just Communicating to Connecting.

- Be in the moment.

When building connections, focus on the moment and stop thinking about what went wrong in the past or your future worries. Just be fully available to the present moment and the shared experience everyone has with one another.

- Be yourself.

Connection only works if there is honest, authentic communication. It doesn't work if you are trying to be something you aren't.

- Be open – whether you feel good or not.

Connecting with others can feel good, sometimes. Stepping out in trust with someone by sharing a painful experience or something you are upset about can be a very powerful way of connecting.

- Show empathy and kindness.

Apathy or harshness shut off connections, as do judgment and criticism. Empathy and kindness are the best soil to grow strong connections in.

- Create a Sense of Trust.

Two ways to build trust are taking accountability and being constant. Trust is a natural result when you do what you say and take ownership of what you do.

- Give before you ask.

Building connections is about adding value to others. Every connection is a give and take, but don't link your give to a take. Give because you want to add value, period.

Types of Connections to Build.

Aside from building personal and professional connections with people, there are a few other types of connections you will want to build as part of your journey to living your vision.

- One connection you want to establish is with your values. Habits change, values and purpose don't. It might seem odd to say you have the intention to sit down and develop a connection to your values. But so few people have ever sat down and wrote out a list of their values and placed those values at the center of their goals. But, by establishing a clearly defended connection to your values, you stay anchored in who you are and what you believe so when times get tough and you need to change direction, you do so from a place of certainty and fear.

- Another connection you will want to establish is with your faith. Prayer is about communication and establishing a relationship. When you connect to your faith, you are making an intentional decision to move into a relationship. Having a Faith Connection is all about identifying what faith means to you, what you have faith IN, and what becomes possible with even greater faith. Faith is not a destination, philosophy, religion, or a thing. Faith is the ability and experience of living with trust and unshakable confidence. Even in the midst of doubts, obstacles, and fears, you will need a Faith Connection to achieve your highest potential, and to authentically express yourself. Building a Faith Connection is to recognize and re-connect with your true power within.

- And finally, a connection to your vision. For the last seven lessons, we have been talking about building and achieving a vision, but have you really connected to it. Have you connected mind, body, spirit, and soul to that vision? Has your vision become a living, breathing thing that you not only communicate about, but you connect with. Until you fully connect to your vision, you will always hold a part of yourself back, and you will not be giving 100% into achieving your vision. You can't give 60% and expect a 100% return.

Never underestimate the empowering effect of human connection. All you need is that one person who understands you completely, believes in you, and makes you feel loved for what you are, to enable you - to unfold the miraculous YOU.

EXERCISES FOR LESSON 8

Exercise 1

By now, you know what to do. Time to connect with our goals.

Take a moment and write each of your goals with the following format from the last lesson:

To will achieve my goal_______________(goal). I will not allow________(obstacle/excuse) to stop me. Instead, I will___________ (action step) so that I can experience the_____ (benefit of the goal). I also accept that the gap___________ (pick one) is a natural part of the growth process and will use the following tool to grow through the gap___________ (add one tool you identified). I will also commit the required resource________ (the one you feel it will take) to achieve this goal. And I will pause and take inventory of ___________________to make sure I have what it takes.

____

____

____

____

____

Exercise 2

Let's take a moment and take inventory of our connections. First, make a list of the five "people" connections in your life or business and which of the five values they bring to the relationship.

    Who: Value:

____

____

____

____

____

Exercise 3

Looking at the list you just completed, ask yourself which relationships need to grow, which need to go, and what values are missing to achieve your vision. We need to be mindful of the people we bring along on our journey and if they are adders or subtracters to our success. This is about resource management, not the individual.

* If you choose to add someone and don't know who they are, simply add the value you want to add.

Grow	Go	Add

Exercise 4

If connections are about giving before getting, take a moment, and list three "building blocks" that you feel are your strengths in building new connections.

Exercise 5

Looking back over the last eight lessons, do you feel equipped to follow through on your goals and achieve your Vision? What's different now than before? Take a minute and write your response below.

LESSON NINE
PUTTING IT ALL TOGETHER

*WITHOUT KNOWLEDGE ACTION IS USELESS,
AND KNOWLEDGE WITHOUT ACTION IS FUTILE.*

What do you really want out of life? Is it a higher position in your career, a more loving relationship, or your own successful business? We are wired to want to "do better." That's why growth is so addictive. No matter what you're pursuing, self-improvement goals are a critical part of your progress and happiness. But all too often, our efforts at self- improvement fail. We aren't sure which direction to head in, so we end up stumbling around, hoping we'll just happen upon the job, relationship, or life we want. If you've ever fumbled through a dark room in search of a light, you know this "tactic" often fails. You are now more equipped than 99% of the people you know outside this group.

Self-improvement ideas and workshops aren't enough. You need to get clear on what you want and have a clearly written actionable outline of what can get you there. We will use this space and time to gather everything you have learned and written into one place.

Goal #1

I will achieve my goal (goal).

I will not allow(obstacle/excuse) to stop me. Instead, I will (action step) so that I can experience the (benefit of the goal).

I also accept that the gap (pick one) is a natural part of the growth process and will use the following tool to grow through the gap (add one tool you identified).

I will also commit the required resource (the one you feel it will take) to achieve this goal. And I will pause and take inventory of to make sure I have what it takes.

The goal is:

____

____

____

____

Three obstacles/excuses that stopped me in the past:

A. ____

____

____

____

B.____

____

____

____

C.____

____

____

Action steps I will take to move past these obstacles/excuses:

A.____

____

____

B.____

____

____

C.____

____

____

____

I understand that setbacks happen to everyone. Three setbacks that I might encounter:

A.____

____

____

B.____

____

____

C.____

____

____

____

I understand that gaps are a natural part of growth. Three gaps that I am prepared to jump are:

A.____

____

____

B.____

____

____

C.____

____

____

I know that the system/habits I will need to develop or continue to develop are:

A.____

____

____

B.____

____

____

C.____

____

____

The resources I need to succeed are abundant, and I will take inventory of those resources by:

A.____

____

____

____

B.____

____

____

____

C.____

____

____

____

To grow these connections, I will need/use along the journey are:

A.____

____

____

____

B.____

____

____

____

C.____

____

____

____

Goal #2

To will achieve my goal (goal).

I will not allow(obstacle/excuse) to stop me. Instead, I will (action step) so that I can experience the (benefit of the goal).

I also accept that the gap (pick one) is a natural part of the growth process and will use the following tool to grow through the gap (add one tool you identified).

I will also commit the required resource (the one you feel it will take) to achieve this goal. And I will pause and take inventory to make sure I have what it takes.

The goal is:

____

____

____

____

Three obstacles/excuses that stopped me in the past:

A.____

____

____

____

B.____

____

____

____

C.____

____

____

____

Action steps I will take to move past these obstacles/excuses:

A. ____

____

____

B. ____

____

____

C. ____

____

____

____

I understand that setbacks happen to everyone. Three setbacks that I might encounter:

A. ____

____

____

B. ____

____

____

C. ____

____

____

I understand that gaps are a natural part of growth. Three gaps that I am prepared to jump are:

A.____

____

____

B.____

____

____

C.____

____

____

I know that the system/habits I will need to develop or continue to develop are:

A. ____

____

____

B.____

____

____

C.____

____

____

The resources I need to succeed are abundant, and I will take inventory of those resources by:

A.____

____

____

B.____

____

____

C.____

____

____

____

To grow the connections, I will need/use along the journey are:

A.____

____

____

B.____

____

____

C.____

____

____

Goal #3

To will achieve my goal (goal).

I will not allow(obstacle/excuse) to stop me. Instead, I will (action step) so that I can experience the (benefit of the goal).

I also accept that the gap (pick one) is a natural part of the growth process and will use the following tool to grow through the gap (add one tool you identified).

I will also commit the required resource (the one you feel it will take) to achieve this goal. And I will pause and take inventory to make sure I have what it takes.

The goal is:

Three obstacles/excuses that stopped me in the past:

A.______________________________________

____

____

____

B.______________________________________

____

____

C.______________________________________

____

____

Action steps I will take to move past these obstacles/excuses:

A.____

____

____

B.____

____

____

C.____

____

____

I understand that setbacks happen to everyone. Three setbacks that I might encounter:

A.____

____

____

B.____

____

____

C.____

____

____

I understand that gaps are a natural part of growth. Three gaps that I am prepared to jump are

A.____

____

____

____

B.____

____

____

____

C.____

____

____

____

I know that the system/habits I will need to develop or continue to develop are

A.____

____

____

____

B.____

____

____

____

C.____

____

____

____

The resources I need to succeed are abundant, and I will take inventory of those resources by:

A.____

____

____

____

B.____

____

____

____

C.____

____

____

____

To grow the connections, I will need/use along the journey are:

A.____

____

____

____

B.____

____

____

____

C.____

____

____

____

My Daily Five

The Daily 5 is simply a series of activities that you do EVERY DAY that are fundamental to your success.

The first step in setting your daily routine is determining what matters to you. You can't prioritize if you don't know your priorities.

If you're not sure of your priorities, ask yourself what I want my Attitude, Health, Family, Thinking, Commitment, Finances, Faith, Relationships, Growth to look like.

With that for context, take a moment to list your Daily Five. Feel free to look back at Lesson One if you need it.

My Daily Five will be:

1.______________________________________

____

____

____

2.______________________________________

____

____

____

3.______________________________________

____

____

____

4.______________________________________

____

____

____

5.______________________________________

____

____

____

Two things to remember: 1) Be flexible daily about how much time you give each activity. 2) Be willing to change and update each activity as you feel called to.

You are never really "done" with personal growth. There is always something to refine and develop and always a new way to learn, change and give back. When this lesson ends, you will become your accountability coach. So now is a perfect time to commit to how you will continue to grow.

I commit to the following:

Daily Activities:

____

____

____

____

Weekly Actives:

____

____

____

____

Monthly Actives:

____

____

____

____

Yearly Actives:

____

____

____

____

Take a moment and reflect on everything you have learned about yourself and about living a bigger, bolder vision of your life. What one thing made this experience "worth it"?

____

____

____

____

You have been on a journey long before you joined this group. You may have never reflected so long and hard on what you wanted in your life before now. So, take a moment and pat yourself on the back to give yourself permission to dream big dreams and take the time to build systems to achieve those dreams.

Start With Vision is not just a book or a workshop. It is a belief that when an individual can fully see and then chooses to live the vision God has placed in them for a bigger, better life, we honor Him. You are called to chase after that vision, and trust in faith that everything you need to achieve it has already been placed within you.

"So, whether you eat or drink or whatever you do,
do it all for the glory of God. "
1 Corinthians 10:31

Did you resonate with the lessons in this book?

If you are wondering… What's Next?

Visit https://www.SusanSullivan.net

If you would like to connect with Susan Sullivan about coaching services, speaking or consulting services email her at Susan@Susan-Sullivan.net

If you would like to become a
Start With Vision Facilitator,
speak to the person that hosted this event or connect

with the author directly at :

Susan@SusanSullivan.net